Productivity:

How To Multiply Your Income A Thousand Fold.

[c] JUSTIN MACDONATUS

Brass Tacks Series

These are books written by experienced professionals in such a way as to make the points as quickly and in as few words as possible.

They are aimed at the man or woman who has thirty minutes to eat and rest in a restaurant or hotel. Or for those who want to gain knowledge even on a short flight or fast the movies for a quick read without resorting to a dictionary. The man at home but takes time out from the primetime news to top up his professional know-how.

Surprisingly such people are in the majority in today's world of hustle and bustle.

In this series, we attempt a marriage between brevity and potency. It is like bringing out the ***sixty-six books*** of the bible in ***six chapters*** without losing the essence.

Contents

"If you want to increase your productivity, you need to pause and take an inventory. Start with your goods and services. Check the impact of your goods and services in times past. Which one is giving your better result in terms of income? Which one do you put in less work but reap more financial returns? They say you do not change a winning formula. Once you have identified the ones that are bringing in good income and the ones that are not, you have to keep up with the good ones and learn to throw away the less productive ones".

Dedication

This book is dedicated my students in the seminary where I teach.

Chapter One

Begin With These

YOU DO NOT CHANGE A WINNING FORMULA

There is really nothing new under the sun. It is a known fact that there is nothing you will do now that somebody else had never done. Heap up a million in a bank. You will nether be neither the first nor the last to save a million. Go on a shopping spree, rest assured that you are not the first to do so.

Before you were born, there have been billionaires in the world. There have been people who achieved much through hard work and smart work. They have discovered formulas for making money and tricks or should we say wisdom for achieving much with less work.

Once you have this information, and understand it, your problem of how to increase income is solved. Do not listen to anything anyone else has to tell you. I am speaking from experience. Increased income actually comes from increased productivity and sales. I guess you know that already.

People say the same thing in many other ways. Some say no food for a lazy man. Why? If the lazy man fails to produce anything eatable or fails to sell something and make enough money to buy food, then he will go hungry. A farmer does not go hungry because when a man sows, he reaps. I could go on with more examples but that will defeat the purpose of the *BRASS TACKS SERIES* which is to be concise and to the point.

So we cannot dismiss the fact that people who produce more goods and services and sell more of them, make more money.

The question however and that I guess is why you are reading this book, is how do I increase my productivity. However, this book is not just interested in increasing your products and making more sales. Instead, we are seriously interested in increasing your income a thousand fold with less work. *Some call it the smart way to increase your income a thousand fold.*

Let me hit the nail on the head. There are a few steps you should take. The first is to;

CROSSCHECK ALL YOU HAVE BEEN DOING.

Albert Einstein is credited with the saying that a person who does the same thing all the time in the same way is a mad man. I know you are not a mad man. A mad man is not thinking of improving income. He is more interested in doing the same thing for the sake of doing it.

If you want to increase your productivity, you need to pause and take an inventory. Start with your goods and services. Check the impact of your goods and services in times past. Which one is giving your better result in terms of income? Which one do you put in less work but reap more financial returns? They say you do not change a winning formula. Once you have identified the ones that are bringing in good income and the ones that are not, you have to keep up with the good ones and learn to throw away the less productive ones.

YOU HAVE TO ALSO CHECK HOW YOU ARE DOING IT.

Is there an area or process where you waste man hours? Some products and services take a lot of time to produce, package, advertise and sell. Some others take less time. You are not in business just to be in business. You are in it to make money and make it abundantly. So find out those that take up a lot of your time because time is money.

CHECK OUT WHAT OTHER PEOPLE ARE DOING

People are out there making money and they use some formulas and products. There is no harm in finding out how they are making it. They do not need to be your competitors. I am not just talking about monitoring your competitors. No I am talking of going out of your way to interview and observe or read about those who are succeeding and why they are succeeding.

This will save you the stress of researching and coming up with fresh formulas. As I said at the outskirts, there is nothing under the law. Also, I am not asking you to do something illegal. I know that most money making products and ideas are either copyrighted or patented. However, you can be an affiliate, franchisee or a licensed learner and innovator. Instead of wasting your time and energy working donkey hours without meaningful result, look for winning formulas and acquire them legitimately.

This is the very same reason why some companies acquire other companies. They are always on the lookout small and obscure companies out there in some corner, making money or with hidden potentials. Then the smart investors pay the price and grab the formulas and products for themselves. I do not recommend this but some unscrupulous ones do what is called hostile takeover which is simple English is acquiring a company when the owners are not willing to part with it. in my opinion, hostile takeovers are bad and I believe criminal in many countries.

There are still more to be done. In the next chapter, I am going to tell what I did to improve my own income by over a thousand fold.

SUMMARY

1. IF YOU WANT TO INCREASE INCOME, DO NOT WORK FOR WORKING SAKE.

2. FIND OUT WHAT IS WORKING FOR YOU AND WHAT IS NOT.

3. FIND OUT WHAT IS WORKING FOR OTHERS TOO.

4.   DO NOT CHANGE A WINNING FORMULA –
INSTEAD COPY IT.

5. PAY FOR NEW IDEAS AND PRODUCTS IF YOU
HAVE TO.

6.   BE BOLD ENOUGH TO THROW AWAY WHAT
IS NOT WORKING.

  AVOID BEING SENTIMENTALLY ATTACHED TO
ANY PARTICULAR PRODUCT OR PROCESS.

Chapter Two

Consider My Own Story

I was once a jack of all trades and master of none. I did not just try. I actually did the following:

Stewarded a church on full time. I had to spend at least eight hours a day inside the church office. I was also on call when the need arose and the need was always there. Our time on evangelism and follow up was not part of it

 I wrote articles for a newsmagazine on part-time. I am a journalist by profession and retired as an editor. When things became financially tough, after I resigned my job to become a full time pastor of a young church, I was forced to proof-read articles sent to me, at odd hours.

Conducted training for church workers. We had workers retreats and seminars where we taught ushers, security personnel and elders what it took to be in their position.

I conducted seminars for pastors and other ministers. Usually a five day, 9-3pm sit in where we diagnose church diseases and how ministers can cure them.

 I authored several books. Instead of me to rest at some week days that I have less to do in the church, I spent my spare time writing slim books, you could call them pamphlets which I still had to hawk myself to make ends meet especially in the first five years of our ministry.

I taught part-time in a seminary. I did not think I would have to teach but there I was, the best student in the class and my Alma matter offered me a teaching job. This opened a floored-gate of opportunities in the ministry. I found myself teaching in more than one seminary at a time.

I distributed and sold most of my books myself. Sometime, I would reach out at six and come home at seven-thirty, in an attempt to reach church bookshops and pastors so that I can talk them into taking some of my books.

I worked as a paid public speaker and motivator. The students I taught in the seminary and those who meet me at the seminars began to invite me to their events and churches to speak. This also began to encroach on my over-loaded time.

I consulted for some pastors who wanted their books written or published. As I began to spread my books, I met pastors who also wanted to write books. Since they could see my books, they began to ask me questions. I not only told them what to do but had to ghost-write for some and edit for some others or merely proof read for yet another group. All of these were time consuming.

I am a husband and father of four on top of it all. This in itself is supposed to be a full time job but for me, it became a part-time thing.

Twenty-four hours in a day was not enough for me. Sometimes, I would leave my home at nine in the morning only to return at about ten in the evening. Some of my clients lived in the other end of the town. My phone kept on ringing and I would get home dog tired. I worked like an elephant but ate like a mosquito.

My bank balance did not reflect my effort. Most times, the account would be in red. I could not provide three balanced meals for my family. My children were always sent out of school. Each day, I would not be home till long after the children had gone to bed. Yet, I was over-working myself.

My health was suffering. I began to be a candidate for the hospitals. Fever today, headache tomorrow. Bills were mounting.

However, one day it occurred to me that I was not putting my training into practice. I was acting like a fool who just took delight in being busy. From the day awareness came to me, I decided to be more professional in the conduct of my affairs.

In the next chapter I will tell you the vital things I did to change my story. Permit me to tell you that me who did not ever have my account in blue ink began to be invited for a chat by the bank manager. The moment I changed my modus operandi, I got to know that banks canvas people to buy into some of their products and services. I moved out of the mass housing districts into the more peaceful and less crowded areas. In a short while, I got cars and began to go by air on some of my long distance journeys. We have not reached where we are going but the going is no longer tough just because I did something very simple which we will talk about in the next chapter.

SUMMARY

I once worked like an elephant.   It did not add to my income.

I tried to do too many things at a time.

I was always out of my home.

I was always tired.

 My children did not get to see me.

 I did some things to harvest a change.

 You too can do the same.

Chapter Three

This Is What I Did

I BEGAN WITH AN OVERVIEW OF MY ACTIVITIES

I sat down with pen and paper. I took an inventory of the things I used to do. What were the services I rendered and the products I sold. How much was I making from each of these?

I not only made a list, I did not trust myself. So I asked some close associates to tell me some of the things they know that I spend my time and money on. That was how I remembered that I used to go and consult for some pastors who needed to write books. I was not an expert but in the land of blind men, the one eyed man is the king.

I ASKED MYSELF SOME BASIC QUESTIONS

What is my priority? Why am I doing all these things? Am I doing them to make a living or just because I have a passion for them or just doing them to keep myself busy and to be seen as busy? I tried to be as honest to myself as I could be. I found that some of the things I was doing, I was doing them just to be seen as Mr. Nice but they took more of my time than the ones that really fetched me more income. As my bills mounted, I told myself that there is a time for everything. A philanthropist has to first make money before he can donate here and there.

I IDENTIFIED THE REAL EARNER IN MY LOT

I found that it was my conferences and seminars that actually brought in more money to me than anything else. So many dead woods were in the basket with no value than weight. Call them bag and baggage. Not only that, the seminars and conferences introduced me to more people in my line of business and one open door led easily to another. This could not be said of the other businesses where repeat orders were not guaranteed. Some time, the seminary would not have enough students for a session so teaching would be suspended. To cut a long story short, found out what to throw away and what to keep.

I ALSO DECIDED TO LOOK AROUND

I was able to see what other people were doing to make money and increase income. In the course of my interviews and search, I found that the only way you can have repeat others well is to deal in something that people would need every day. Since it is a daily need for the people around you, they will surely ask for it again. This cannot be placed on the same pedestal as my books which I had to hawk or market myself most times. I made a mental note that when I need to diversify, I would take pains to look for products that are essential to peoples survival because it is not enough to be ever busy and produce goods and services which no one buys.

I ALSO DISCOVERED SOMETHING STRANGE

I did not keep proper records of my businesses. I had difficulty determining what was earning and what was not. Most of the businesses I just ran out of my pocket and kept the records in my brain. So when I needed them to make sound judgment, I did not have the help.

Please, go through the summary of my discovery below and I will quickly tell you in the next chapter, three vital things I did before launching out again.

SUMMARY

I did not keep good records.

Determining what earned and what not was difficult.

I realized that some of the things I did were time wasters.

Some of my services were not getting repeat orders. That meant that I had to keep knocking on doors.

 I found that I did some things just to please some people.

I found out how others were legitimately making money without much effort.

I needed to focus on my seminars and conferences.

Chapter Four

Three Vital Things You Must Do

Soon after I identified the real income earners and the time wasters, I did the following:

INNOVATION

I took a close look at my seminars and conferences. I asked myself, what am I doing that I ought not to be doing? What was really bringing in the money in the conference? What can be thrown away without losing value or income?

To help me again, I pen and paper. I did an audit of my processes. I found that I normally do the following;

Determine what to speak on.

Make contact with my prospective venues.

Appoint a chairman and raise an organizing committee.

Print fliers and materials needed for the advertising and the conference itself.

Pre-register people for the conference.

See to technical issues at the venue including equipment, cleanliness, etc

Arrange for catering services.

Once I had these on paper, I began to ask myself, is there any of these items I can improve on or introduce to earn more income? is there something I am supposed to do that I was not doing?

To cnable me answer these questions, I did not have the resources to hire a consultant. So I decided to do what I could on my own.

Among other things, I decided that I could introduce the given of awards to those who merit them on the last day of my programs. I also realized that I could group all participant into a body through which we can continue to relate with ourselves beyond the conferences. I created social media groups for easier and cheaper   communication. I used to conduct the seminars for five days at a stretch; I realized that I could do the same conference for three days. This meant that I could now do the same conference twice instead of once in a week as I formally did. That surely led to increased productivity and increased income.

DELEGATION

Next, I asked myself why I was not involving others in what I was doing. I did most of these things myself. I would single handedly research and determine what was to be talked about at the meetings. I would run around for the printings and then travel to talk with people at the prospective venue. I discovered that I could delegate almost all aspects of what I was doing. So I began a search for credible men to whom I can outsource my jobs. With time I found that some of my people even did better than me. Why earn only from your effort when you can earn more from the effort of others.

REPLICATION

I found out that I could do ten or more program per week.

I transferred most of my services to an institution and employed more capable hands. I depersonalized my services so that others can handle them. Today, we do up to twenty conferences per week in several countries!

We have found that we have great productivity potential. Our seminars have been innovated in a way that they can hold in any part of the world. All we need to do is increase the number of people handling our affairs.

Doing these things have:

I increased our income in multiples.

It has given me more time for my family.

It has enabled me to stay focused on what is important.

It has increased my personal productivity.

SUMMARY

I found ways to add value to what we were doing.

I found a way to involve others.

We shortened the production time.

We introduced some things others were doing and which we were not doing.

We increased our volume of trade.

We were not afraid of involving others.

Innovation, delegation and replication are vital to increased output and income.

Chapter Five

Ten Things You Must Avoid

The other chapters focused on things you should do to increase productivity and by implication increase income. This chapter focuses on things you must avoid if income will not nose-dive. Chief among these salient points are:

DO NOT WORK WITHOUT A PLAN

They say failing to plan is tantamount to planning to fail. Having a plan is setting goals, targets, timelines and clear-cut procedures for reaching the set goals and targets. Having a plan is making sure in advance that everyone knows who is to do what and how it is done within given time. It is to define responsibility so that people can take risks knowing that they will not only be held accountable for their actions but rewarded for their results. .

Good plans save time, remove confusion, improve efficiency and increase productivity in so many ways. When we have no plans, productivity decreases and so too income. Therefore have a plan for all you do.

AVOID GIVING EXCUSES

This is nothing but having a good reason for not doing what you suppose to do. We invent reasons to justify inaction. When we do nothing, we produce and sell nothing. In turn, we have no profits to make. When a plan is put in place, we must work hard and be disciplined enough to see that the said plans are put into action. Those who give excuse, almost always have acceptable reasons for doing nothing but no matter our reasons, it cannot change the fact that nothing was produced and nothing sold.

AVOID PROCRASTINATION

This is the younger brother of excuse. In my own words, procrastination is simply postponing what has to be done now to another time. It does nothing but achieves the same result as when we do nothing due to our ability to give long excuses. A man who wants to improve his income must take action.

AVOID GREEDINESS

This is what makes us want to go into many businesses at the same time when we cannot even run one well. We become jack of all trades and master of none. We put our hand into so many pies that our two eyes cannot oversee the much we are doing. More times, it pays to stay focused.

AVOID DELAYS IN DELIVDERY

For income to improve the individual must strive do away with delays in the supply chain. Production processes as well as delivery mechanism should be reviewed from time to time with a view to uprooting causes of delay. When delays occur, both machines and man sit idle.

AVOID PRIDE

This can stop a man or management from humbling himself enough to learn from others, especially those doing better than him or his company, in the market place. We know that pride can make a man shut his mouth when he should be asking for help or seat down to study under people who know more than him and a closed mouth is a closed destiny.

AVOID TIME TAKING HOBBIES

Nothing stumps productivity like time taking hobbies. This is more pronounced among youths who follow things like the ENGLISH PREMIER LEAGUE with a great passion. I know golfers who spend more time on the golf course, to mention another example that they do in their business place.

It is not a bad thing to have a hobby but sport or whatever, should not over-throw your source of income in terms of priority.

DO NOT ALLOW PHONES CONTROL YOU

Telephones have a way of intruding into work schedules that human visitors do not have. I guess telephones still enjoy celebrity status worldwide. The same man or woman that when he or she comes calling physically will be stopped at the gate or at the secretary's table easily bulldozes his way into the office of the chief executive because he or she is using a cell phone. We are now in a situation where anyone with a telephone can reach us when we do not want to be reached! We have now become reactionary victims of telephones. The matter is worse when we have cranky callers. We need to find a way to control the phones instead of them controlling us if we want to increase productivity and income.

LIMIT OR STOP EARLY CALLERS

In the same vein, we need to limit early callers. Some people call when you just woke up or just entered your offices. They do not even give you time to look through the diary to know what your timelines and priorities are for the day. Most of these callers, call for personal matters that do not add to your corporate results. They book no appointment because if they did, there is no way you would have allowed them to come calling when you are yet to even have your breakfast talk less of being ready for the business day.

They should be stopped before they stop you from reaching your corporate goals.

HAVE A PREFERENCE FOR TEXT MESSAGES

They are shorter and easier to read. Because they cost money per letter, writers are forced to be direct and specific. Nothing can be more time saving that this and we know that time is money.

In conclusion, permit me to say that it is not enough to know what needs o be done but that one must develop the will and discipline to see that what has to be done is done and what has to be avoided is avoided.

FEAR

Fear is to be feared. It does not allow a man to take risks or try out new ideas. It makes a social recluse out of us. We fear so many things. Will I make it? Can I cope with the known competition? What if people do not buy? We ask over a million questions that only help to emphasize our fears.

A man that is afraid does not step out of his home when others are venturing out.

A wise person will learn from soldiers. Encased in fear and obvious danger, they rush out to battle! They know full well that to stand idle is to be defeated. An entrepreneur has no business with fear. His reward is for labor and risk taken. Therefore he must step out and take his chances, leaving fear out of it.

Chapter Six

The Matter In A Nutshell

What problem did we talk about? We addressed the pressing issue of how to increase income a thousand fold. This presupposes that the enquirer already had some income going for him or her. What we need to do was increasing it at all and increase it a thousand fold.

What did we recommend? We said first, find out what works best for you. Sometimes a man might have his hands in so many things but only one or two are money spinners. The rest could just be things he did just to be seen as busy or genuinely keep him busy. Money has nothing to do with them at all.

To find out what works for you also presupposes that you have been keeping records which most small scale businesses and individuals rarely do. Go through your records and locate your income. Which one gives you fewer hassles and earns big? Identify and put it in a cart.

Next, we recommended that you brush up that business, thing or service to make it more appealing to the buying public than it had been in the past. Call it innovation. Find out what you can throw away. Find out what you can add. Give more value with the new improved product or service. Find out how you can serve a new product at lower cost and better appeal.

That done, you go to the next step.

People your money spinner. Bring more people into the work. Make it easy for people to come into what you are doing. Mass produce if you have to. Automate if can. Whatever you do, do not depend on your labor alone. Let there be a surge of the workforce. Franchise, get affiliates or get more sales men involved but involve more people you must. Increase what you had been earning from one spot into a thousand fold or more.

Now, let me tell you this – that is the reason why people own chain stores. The more the sales outlet you have or the more sales you make of your product or service, the cheaper the cost of production becomes because you have to buy in bulk and a major advantage of that is that the raw materials and labor too, becomes cheaper. It even becomes better if you market a generic product or service that can be purchased by just anybody.

The product or service must be good and tested. You must have test ran it over time and know that this one works. You do not just pick anyone of the things you do and start to boost or push it. it must be the one you know for sure that the market is buying. As I said in my own case, out of over ten things I did for a living, I found that only one was rake in good money. So I concentrated on it. After improving on it that is! With that one move, we:

We stopped wasting money on dead or dying horses.

We began to specialize in some areas of the process involved in that particular service.

We bought our materials in bulk thus lowering our costs.

We improved on our delivery services cutting out delays.

We found a way to have repeat orders, so we sold more.

We trained others to do what we were doing.

We became focused instead of dissipating energy on things that did not pay.

We created new markets.

We learnt to do impact assessment so as to know how to improve.

Of course, to enable us keep track of our activities and results, we learnt to keep better records.

All these led to what increase productivity and increased income. We got a thousand fold increases when we increased the tempo of work and efficiency a thousand fold.

You can do the same. Believe me: nothing under the sun is impossible.

EPILOGUE

If you have read this book and have some questions to ask or comments, the author will be quite glad to answer or receive your comments.

Write to the author at:

newochei@gmail.com.

OTHER BOOKS BY JUSTIN MCDONATUS

1. One Surprisingly Cheap Flight To Wealth

www.ingramcontent.com/pod-product-compliance
Lightning Source LLC
Chambersburg PA
CBHW020714180526
45163CB00008B/3083